SO YOU'RE

70!

Mike Haskins & Clive Whichelow

Illustrations by Ian Baker

summersdale

SO YOU'RE 70!

First published in 2008
Reprinted 2009, 2010, 2012
This edition copyright © Mike Haskins and Clive Whichelow, 2013

Illustrations by Ian Baker

Summersdale Publishers Ltd
46 West Street
Chichester
West Sussex
PO19 1RP
UK

www.summersdale.com

Printed and bound in China

ISBN: 978-1-84953-440-6

Substantial discounts on bulk quantities of Summersdale books are available to corporations, professional associations and other organisations. For details contact Nicky Douglas by telephone: +44 (0) 1243 756902, fax: +44 (0) 1243 786300 or email: nicky@summersdale.com.

To... Tom

From... love from Di

x x x x x x x

INTRODUCTION

Oh dear, 70! At 50 you could kid yourself you were still quite young; and compared to 70 you were! Even at 60 you weren't quite retired, but 70 – that's pretty old! You're older than Israel, Sri Lanka and Biffo the Bear.

You're now even too old to look forward to a bus pass, and you'll probably now never swim with dolphins – unless one finds its way into your walk-in bath.

But at least you're someone the rest of the family looks up to – especially when they want to borrow some money.

And if you wake up from an afternoon nap sweating from a nightmare about being surrounded by multiple Grim Reapers, don't worry; it's just your lovely little grandchildren in their hoodies demanding yet another hand-out.

But it's not all bad news – you're still younger than Bruce Forsyth, Superman, and the speaking clock!

So, you're 70 – so what!

THE BASIC MYTHS ABOUT TURNING 70

You're a grumpy old git – really? No work, free travel, people giving you their seat on crowded buses... what's to be grumpy about?

You're into your second childhood – not unless you count sleeping in the day and needing the toilet in the middle of the night

YOUR LIFE WILL NOW CONSIST OF...

*Trying to find your glasses
(try top of head or dangling
from string round neck)*

Feeding the entire bird population of your neighbourhood

DRESS CODE FOR THE OVER-70S – SOME DOS AND DON'TS

Don't think because you're at home all day you don't have to make an effort. You may end up absent-mindedly popping to the shops in your pyjamas

Do try to retain some dignity. Miniskirts and high heels just won't look right – especially on you men

TIPS ON HOW TO APPEAR YOUNGER THAN YOU ACTUALLY ARE

If bits of your body are beginning to sag, hang upside down while having your photograph taken, then invert the resulting picture when you show it to people

If you can't afford Botox, Polyfilla makes a cheap and cheerful substitute for filling in those wrinkles

THE MAIN EVENTS IN YOUR LIFE IT'S LESS EASY TO LOOK FORWARD TO

Going out, then forgetting where you live

Unexpectedly finding you need your neighbours to help you out of the bath

CONVERSING WITH YOUNG PEOPLE (PART 1)

What you say and
what they hear

'I beg your pardon?' =
*'Please speak directly into
my face as loud as you can
while generally treating me
like a complete idiot'*

'That reminds me...' =
'Let me once again tell you
the entire history of my life
in extraordinary detail'

'So who's top of the
pops then?' =
'I was around when Edison
invented the phonograph'

A LIST OF CONTROVERSIAL OPINIONS YOU WILL NOW BE EXPECTED TO HOLD

'"Illegal immigrant" means anyone who arrived in this country after the Angles and Saxons'

'Pensioners should be allowed to carry guns for self-protection'

'Groups of youths found hanging around after dark should be collected by the military and used for target practice'

CONVERSING WITH YOUNG PEOPLE (PART 2)

What they say and
what you hear

'Would you like my
bus seat?' =
'Sit down before you fall
down you poor old sod'

'I bet you've seen a few changes in your time' = 'So what were horse-drawn buses and rickets like?'

'Do you want any help packing your shopping?' = *'You'll do yourself a mischief trying to lift that large jar of Marmite'*

THINGS YOU CAN NOW GET AWAY WITH THAT YOU COULDN'T PREVIOUSLY

Using your false teeth
to crimp a pie crust

Suddenly going deaf when approached by charity collectors

**THINGS
THAT YOU WILL
TAKE A SUDDEN
INTEREST IN**

*Any new tablets that a friend
has just been prescribed
by the doctor*

The obituaries column – just to see who you've outlived today

Places where you can keep warm without it costing you a penny

HOORAY!
THINGS YOU'LL
NEVER HAVE TO
DO AGAIN

Work!

Consider what clothes might be in fashion

Feel that you're wasting the doctor's time

BOO! THINGS YOU WON'T BE DOING AGAIN

Having candles on your birthday cake correctly matching your age

Being hired on the basis of your looks rather than your ability

SHATTERING MOMENTS TO COME SOON

You drop off mid-conversation when talking to yourself

You discover that the rest
of the bowls team are
younger than you

You realise the bath isn't filling up because you've forgotten to close the door on the side

You refuse your favourite food because it's 'a bit hard to chew'

BEING 70 IS...

... meeting someone at bingo rather than meeting someone and – bingo!

... *when short pants are your summer breathing pattern rather than your summer wardrobe*

*... being as old as the hills
but having a bit of difficulty
walking over them*

... being a bit long in the tooth – it should be a bit long in the teeth, but that's ageing for you

THINGS YOU SHOULD NOT HAVE IN YOUR HOME

Go-faster stripes on the side of your Zimmer frame

Underwear from your youth still in regular service

YOUR NEW
OUTLOOK
ON LIFE

*You're as old as you feel –
unfortunately, some days
you feel about 98*

It's too late to give up drinking or smoking now

*You've seen it all before –
although admittedly last
time you saw it, it was in
slightly sharper focus*

YOUR NEW
WEEKLY
HIGHLIGHTS

*Having a nice Sunday
morning drive when all those
young idiots are still in bed*

Spending the whole
weekend doing the
giant crossword

Despite having all week to do your shopping, saving it all till Saturday morning so you can drive the people who have to work all week crazy!

THINGS YOU WILL DESPERATELY TRY TO AVOID

*Relatives who have taken
a sudden interest in the
contents of your will*

Watching the TV with the volume turned up to maximum

THINGS YOU WON'T BE DOING ON HOLIDAY ANY MORE

Waking up in the morning fuzzy-headed and not remembering where the hell you are (though on second thoughts...)

Playing beach volleyball

HOW TO BE
PHILOSOPHICAL
ABOUT BEING 70

It's not 70.
It's 58 plus VAT

*Antiques are always
more valuable than any
more recently produced
equivalents*

REASONS TO
BE CHEERFUL

If your laughter lines are anything to go by you've had a fabulous fun-filled life. Seventy not out!

Your teeth are looking in better shape than ever before – so what if they spend all night in a glass next to your bed?

If you're interested in finding out more about our books, find us on Facebook at Summersdale Publishers and follow us on Twitter at @Summersdale.

www.summersdale.com